What I Know Now

A Guide for Young Men Looking for Direction

BY

Chris Finley

What I Know Now

© Copyright 2024 - All rights reserved.

The content contained within this book may not be reproduced, duplicated or transmitted without direct written permission from the author or the publisher.

Under no circumstances will any blame or legal responsibility be held against the publisher, or author, for any damages, reparation, or monetary loss due to the information contained within this book, either directly or indirectly.

Legal Notice:

This book is copyright protected. It is only for personal use. You cannot amend, distribute, sell, use, quote or paraphrase any part, or the content within this book, without the consent of the author or publisher.

Disclaimer Notice:

Chris Finley

Table of Contents

Chris Finley

Introduction

"What I know now." Just like the book title says. This thought came to me while I was thinking over a hot cup of green tea. Looking out the window at palm trees swaying back and forth in the beach breeze of my California second-floor apartment, I was reminiscing and reflecting on what I should have kept as a priority in my life. Believe it or not, we all have a purpose: to figure out what we should be doing and what we should've learned by now. These priorities, if I knew what I know now, could point me in the right direction. When it comes to love and life for men, these factors can be listed as such: career, money, and women. Most men have their structure reversed, such as money, women, careers or women, money, and careers, which is the worst priority structure you can have as a man. Not that women shouldn't be in your priority structure, but that women are human. You can't always count on other human beings to ensure your destiny/priorities.

But regardless of whatever commonality there is, the woman is always at the bottom, no matter how you look at it. A woman needs to look up to you–if she doesn't look up to you, she can't respect you. That is one of the main reasons people break up and why people stay in long-term marriages or relationships. If you don't respect your partner, you won't stay with them for long. If you have different values, you have different thoughts, feelings, and actions. How do you feel about food, how people are treated, about work, or do you care about how your home looks or how we care for others? All these are rooted in our value systems. Therefore, our actions are derived from our values. So if you don't share values with someone, you're not going to be in a relationship with them long-term. Which is why most relationships don't make it to long-term status.

If you don't respect the company you are working for or the supervisor you work under, you won't stay there long, either. You won't be able to stay with that company or work under that supervisor for more than three years. Usually, in the first year, it's the excitement of a new job that keeps you getting up every morning to go to work. In the second year, you're trying to find solutions that will work for you—things that are comfortable for you.

If there are any rewards in the job that you look up to, maybe you are missing them. By the third year, if you have not found any of these rewards you start to go against your own value system about what you want in a job, and you would trick yourself into wanting to stay at the job and look up to the company you are working for. Therefore, if you want a job or want to hire someone who is going to stay long-term at your company, your best bet is to find someone who shares your values. This is also true when it comes to meeting someone and being in a relationship.

It's unfortunate for the nice guy who means well in his life. His priorities are different from everyone else's—women, money, career or maybe women, career, money. No matter how you look at it, women should not be your first priority in life. Men who cherish such values and place a woman on top of their pyramid are a low form of mankind. And they will never really succeed in life because they put women first. I believe that when you do this, you end up creating a vice for yourself, just like drugs or alcohol, because the guy sees nothing else but those two things. And without one or the other, his mind becomes idle because that's all he knows. And without it, he can't move on to that new adventure or the great success he knows is there.

When you're 25 years old, you can be an idiot, it's no problem. Even when you're out in a job search, they are like, "Well, you don't have any experience and you're kind of clueless." Yah! Yah! You're young, it's no problem. That's what young people are like, but they are full of potential. Okay, now, you're the same person you were in your 30s and people aren't so thrilled about you at that point. What the HELL have you been doing for the last 10 years?

Well, I'm just as clueless as I was when I was 22. Yeah, but you're not 22, You're an old infant and that's an ugly thing, an old infant. So, part of the reason you choose your damn sacrifice is because the sacrifice is inevitable, but at least you get to choose it.

–Jordan Peterson

Chapter 1: Priorities

The *Oxford Dictionary*'s definition of "priorities" is "the fact or condition of being regarded or treated as more important" or "something that is valued higher than another." For instance, no one ever told me what my priorities should be when I was younger, before I was a man with responsibilities. Like most young men who lack guidance or understanding of what should or should not be more important to them, things sort of fell into place. When I was in high school, all I knew was girls first, thanks to my raging hormones and puberty. If there was a girl involved, everything else flew out the window, even my grades. However, this is the pinnacle, during a time when I had to learn discipline and was eventually taught by older men in my family, such as my dad and uncle, who had been there and taught me to have self-control and an understanding of how getting good grades first can potentially lead to being exposed to more girls my age. And they were right—it was called college, along with a taste of freedom.

My goal? Prioritize my grades and put the fun of hanging out with friends to meet girls during high school last on my list of things to do. This way of thinking helped me get into college. Once I got to college, I had no guidance to tell me what to put first—I had already practiced it in high school. It just took a little bit more discipline this time without my parents there, telling me what to do.

But all I knew when I was a teenager was that my priority was to attend class and, at the very least, complete high school. That was my main, if only, goal. I could decide what I want to do later. It was also common where I grew up to marry your first girlfriend from high school, if you happened to have one, which made things harder and would change the course of your life forever, your hopes and dreams dashed. Sadly, for some of us, our parents didn't really talk to us about what we should be doing or what we should want to be when we grew up. Mostly because they didn't know much about life, careers, or the first purchases a young adult should make. For instance, I was unaware that becoming a doctor involved a huge variety of specialties within the profession. When I was a child, the first image that came to mind when someone expressed a desire to become a doctor or when I was asked if I wanted to be one was a man who examined patients who were ill and had to perform surgery. I had no idea that there were different kinds of medical professions—general practitioners, pathologists, urologists, dermatologists—you get my point.

It wasn't until my senior year of college that I learned all this. Maybe I would have prioritized my post-high-school plans if I had known about these alternative paths to becoming a doctor. It's unfortunate because I would have been skilled at providing tangible assistance to others. But our parents did the best they could to give us what they knew and to steer us in the right direction. Their top priorities seemed to be to prevent us from getting killed, going to jail, being kidnapped, and starving to death. I know it sounds funny, but it's true. Back then, no one gave any thought to what priorities you should have; these were lessons you had to learn on your own.

To be completely honest, I initially hung out with a group of guys that I knew were not appropriate for me. I recall developing a bad attitude seemingly out of nowhere. I was constantly angry and thought that everyone was against me. There was one incident that occurred when I was a high-school student. The group of guys I was hanging out with was in line; we were holding our trays to go through the buffet. Unexpectedly, a large-framed student from our class cut in front of one of the guys in my group, who was two people in front of me. I confronted him about his rude behavior, even though I was the third person behind them, and he made no attempt to apologize. He approached me by taking two steps and asking, "What did you say?" Before I realized it, I had already swung with a right hook to his jaw. His lip started to bleed; he backed up and walked away quietly.

The tension from that incident had everyone in the cafeteria surprised at what I did. However, the guys I was with radiated more of a "good job, dude, let him know who he is messing with" vibe to me.

Males are competitive, whether we are friends or not. When a group of young boys gets together, the testosterone levels rise, making it difficult for us to make decisions using our brains. It's as if we want to establish our masculinity and feel that we deserve this "membership" in the group among the other guys. I suppose you could say that when a group of men get together, they typically come to an understanding about who is the Alpha and who deserves membership in the group.

There is undoubtedly one guy in the group that everyone looks up to, whether it's obvious who it is or not.

According to research by MU anthropology professor Mark Flinn, testosterone levels in men rise when they triumph over rivals or strangers, but they usually remain the same when they compete against friends. When I first got the chance to move away from home, I joined the military. Being on my own was exciting, and I could see myself being able to support myself and do anything I wanted to do with my life. I had so many ideas of what I wanted in my life and what I wanted it to be like. As I progressed through each stage of adulthood, I had to learn the hard way about priorities. I had to learn to pay bills first when I only got paid twice a month, even though I'd bought the car I'd always wanted. Of course, that also meant paying for gas and car insurance. It took me about two years to realize this after constant late payments and later getting a car repossessed. My commanding officer spoke with me about prioritizing what's important when I get paid. I was reckless when it came to money. I wanted what I wanted when I wanted it. For some strange reason, I had this idea that I could take care of whatever bills I had later. What I wanted now was more important. So, rather than pay my bills I was going to see a concert or buying a new toy for my car. With this type of mindset, I kept pushing back payments until I was ready or felt like I had the things I wanted.

It can be very embarrassing when your friends are driving their cars, and you are not because you prioritized spending money on yourself first and everything else came second. Luckily for me, I would eventually meet and be able to surround myself with guys who were more responsible with money than I was. It's true what they say: "Show me your friends, and I'll show you your future." And you should always surround yourself with people who are doing better than you at the things you want to obtain or who have the same goals as you, such as becoming rich or getting an education. If it hadn't been for the guys I hang out with, I wouldn't know half the stuff I learned when it came to prioritizing my life and managing my money. Hanging out with people who have lesser goals than you will lower you to their realm, making you have more in common with them, rather than raising yourself up with friends you look up to. In other words, "misery loves company," as they say.

Having Direction

If you want to understand where you should be in life, you have to have some type of direction. Understand what it takes to get where you want to be. You should have a blueprint of what you want and what it will take to get there. A blueprint can be used as a tool to guide you to where you want to be and how you want to get there. It will give you a better understanding of what obstacles you may have to face to get where you want to be. Think of a blueprint as a timeline of what you need to accomplish to reach your goals.

If you want to build an empire, stay single. I get a lot of guys who tell me, "What do you do for interaction?" I'm lonely. But guess what: Entrepreneurship is a very lonely road. Success is hard. I have a solution for all you guys. If you're bored, you're lonely, and you miss your girlfriend, buy a dog!

–Vegas Dave

Chapter 2: Being Single

Adjusting to being single, or recently divorced, isn't as easy when you're older. I don't want to be the creepy older guy still going to clubs trying to pick up girls, dressed as if he's still stuck in a 2004 hip-hop video. I sometimes look at *GQ* and other magazines and observe other guys around me who are my age, living the single man's life, while reading articles about how to dress and being single in your 40s. "The times change, and if you don't change with them, you get left behind" (Bradley Walsh, n.d.).

When I shopped for clothes, I didn't buy anything new or expensive. I learned from the many articles I read about men's fashion (that sometimes included advice from women) as to where to buy new, trendy clothing. I learned to shop in the clearance section or to find clothing that was on sale. Oh, this is how so many women come out of clothing stores with a ton of clothes and barely break $100 on three or four outfits. But men can get away with a lot more. Say I buy two pairs of jeans and three or four shirts. I already have four outfits.

Or maybe two vintage t-shirts, one polo shirt, one button-down shirt, and two pairs of jeans–one dark and one light. That's less than $100 for four different outfits. Grooming is another way to keep up with the times and save money. Instead of spending $25–30 on one haircut, I learned how to cut my own hair, a good road map to start with if you're not sure how you want it styled or cut. So maybe you go to a barber once to have him cut your hair the way you like. From there you just maintain what he has done, then every two weeks you cut your own hair. It's easy.

In addition, I can't stress enough about male hygiene and not letting yourself go. I know when you were with your ex, it was easy to be accepted as who you were; as long as you brought home the bacon, she allowed you to let yourself go. But, unfortunately, it's time to start taking care of yourself—especially if you want to attract that cute lady you see every morning in the elevator on your way to work who gets off on the 4th floor of your building. Not only that, but cleaning yourself up really sticks it to your ex when she sees how clean and maintained you are without her. You might want to make her jealous and let her know you don't need her. You want her to think you're doing great without her in your life. That, my friend, is revenge.

Chris Finley

The mistake I made after my relationship break-up was I wore how sad I was about the break-up on my sleeve. I had moved and let myself go, barely smiling when people she knew saw me. One incident I remember was, after graduating from college, I continued working for a well-known department store in my area as the store security while figuring out what I wanted to do next with my life and getting over a breakup. I was working at the store one day when my ex came shopping, looking at clothes with her new boyfriend. My heart dropped. I looked a mess—I hadn't had a haircut in three months and I had gained weight. I thought that showing her sadness was what I was supposed to do, and then she would feel sorry for me and realize how hurt I was; then she would come back and give me another chance. Remember: I was the guy who listened to Emo rock music constantly during that time, when bands such as Dashboard Confessional and My Chemical Romance were big. Boy, what a big mistake I made that day, showing the ex how I felt, because it didn't make her want me back. The only thing it did was boost her ego. I can say this because we happened to reconnect a few years later. Against all odds, my ex-girlfriend— who was also my college sweetheart—and I became friends. Of course, after years had passed and we were both over what had happened to us, we were able to laugh about what we did wrong to hurt each other. I asked her about the day she came into the department store where I worked with her new guy and when she saw me there looking depressed. She told me, "Honestly, I felt good you were hurting. I wanted you to realize that it was all your fault, and the look of depression on your face didn't make me want you more. It made me feel good that we weren't together anymore, and I had made the right decision to break up with you."

So, guys, I know that in movies and TV shows you have a happy ending when the girl comes back once she sees how miserable the guy is over the breakup, but that's not reality. That's why you want to look your best the next time you run into your ex accidentally. To quote an antiperspirant deodorant commercial: "Never let them see you sweat."

That's why maintaining your appearance and keeping up with grooming are a good idea, even when you're single. These days, Target or Wal-Mart have plenty of men's products available to help keep you fresh in every manly way. They have whole sections dedicated to grooming for the modern man, from skin, body, and facial-hair products.

Another factor you might want to consider maintaining as a single man is your health. I know it's easy to just stop at a Jack-in-the-Box drive-thru window and order two bacon ultimate cheeseburgers, but if you count calories per serving, you've got 930 $\times 2 = 1{,}860$, and that's a lot of calories for one burger. Be aware of what you eat now that the ball and chain (your ex) is gone. The worst thing you could do is give her the satisfaction that your health is deteriorating, you're overweight, and you can barely make it up a flight of stairs. You want to prove her wrong by being the best version of yourself. One move you can make is to sign up for a cooking class. An added bonus with taking a cooking class as a single man is that you might meet someone new. Most women like taking cooking classes to learn new recipes, and nine times out of ten, one of those women is gonna want you to try the food she cooked. That is a great way to meet someone new and become the type of man who can take care of himself.

I wish I understood time a little bit more. I mean, the value of it. I don't think I quite understood that back then. And I think it's particularly, like, I think I wasted a lot of time kinda like chasing girls or like, you know, just. And for what that meant for me, not meaning, like, I was sleeping around. Meaning that it was too important to me. Like that relationship was too important to me. Like to have that, when I needed to be about chasing me. I needed to chase this!

–Mahershala Ali

Chapter 3: Priorities

When I turned 21, I was laser-focused on what the next style was and being with the prettiest girl. All I cared about was who saw me and how I looked to other guys my age. Trying to look cool, be cool, and chase girls was a waste of time; I'd have done better to focus on myself. If I had learned this sooner, it would have done me a world of good. All the money I spent buying nice clothes to look good in front of girls, and the money I spent driving a nice car so I could pick up girls. Turns out it was all a waste because none of that stuff is with me now. Even the girls I tried to impress are gone. It was only recently that I read an article that broke down how much I would have now if I had been more disciplined with my money as a young man. For instance, if I had invested my money into an average mutual fund during my 20s, when I started my first job—say, one with a "good" long-term return that is annualized for 10 years or more at 8–10%, I could have close to $29–30K saved for myself.

I'm not saying the time I spent chasing girls or hanging out was a total waste, but if I had paid more attention to the amount of time spent doing those things, I'd be much better off. Knowing what I know now, I'd have done better focusing on myself to ensure a better future as an adult. I would have read more books, played more sports, and listened to older, successful men instead of acting first and thinking I knew what life was all about. As a young man, I wanted to live fast. When men are young, we think we have it all figured out: women, cars, and money. Just like most young men, I was no different in my views that, as a man, I could take good care of myself. One lesson I learned was to drink less and take chances—approaching an attractive woman or standing in front of people and singing karaoke—sober, regardless of how embarrassed you are when confronting your fears. A real man has character, and the best way to build character is to do things you always wanted to do but have never done before sober.

At that time, I didn't realize my 20s, 30s, and 40s would be the best time to be a man. Making the mistakes I made were gifts from the universe—or God himself—whether it was problems with the law or bad behavior at school or work or just being out and about.

All those life experiences we men face are meant to happen to make us better men. I'm not saying we don't regret those things we went through in life, but it does shape us into being the men we are today. These are the years you really get to live life with the full potential of being a good man. I felt as if the world was my oyster and I could get into any career or adventure I wanted to. I wanted to travel, go to different states or countries. Experience things I've only heard of or saw on television. I would advise any young man who has just finished high school or college to explore the world, if not the country. See what you can accomplish. Something my mother used to tell me after I left home, fresh out of high school, every time I called, was, "Don't be of the world but in the world." I think what she meant was don't try to be wrapped up in everything the world has to offer; live in it and be part of it.

Chapter 4: Fitness

As I got older, into my early 40s, I had stopped being active and all I was doing was going to work every day and eating takeout. I was becoming set in my ways. This is when I noticed my metabolism slowed down and I started to gain weight. A close friend of mine, who was a few years older than I was, had gone through the same transition. He suggested I start a workout routine because the weight I was gaining will get harder to take off as I get older if I'm not active. So, instead of going hard in the gym as if I was on the high-school football team in my teens again, I kept a light cardio routine where I'd go running, hiking, or jogging on the weekends, usually on a Saturday or Sunday morning. Either I would meet up with a close friend or one of my lady friends—and doing fitness activities on a date is scientifically proven to build attraction. If you are getting to know a woman you just met, meeting her for a fitness date is a great way to win her over.

It increases your emotional bond with each other. "Such behavior creates nonverbal matching, or mimicry, which benefits you both" (Stel & Vonk, 2010). "Nonverbal mimicry helps people feel emotionally attuned with one another, and those who experience or engage in it tend to report greater feelings of having 'bonded' with their partner. Exercising together provides an opportunity to create connections, benefiting both your health and your relationship with your new partner" (DiDonato, 2014).

In addition to meeting girls, research has indicated that physical activities like jogging or hiking provide health benefits that include reduced risk of cancer, increased insulin sensitivity, lower cholesterol levels, improved bone density, reduced inflammation, and reduced risk of cardiovascular disease. Not to mention the mental benefits, which show an improvement in mood and reduced risk of depression and anxiety.

When you maintain your health as an older man, you don't have to go to the gym hitting weight like a madman. I recommend doing the basics to maintain a good, muscular physique. Deadlift, for example, is a total body exercise that can help you maintain your overall body strength as well as improve your posture and help reduce the risk of back injury. Not that you want to go heavy, but do just enough weight to allow you to max at 10 reps. According to a study published in the *Journal of Strength & Conditioning*, deadlifts activate many of the large muscle groups in the lower as well as the upper body, including the gluteus maximus, hamstrings, quadriceps, abdominals, and latissimus dorsi (lats) (Farley, 1995). Another good exercise to do as an older man who wants to maintain a good physique is the military press, which is a great full-body workout. The military press hits the shoulders, triceps, upper chest, and upper-back muscles, which carry the majority of motion in your upper body. However, your core and lower-body muscles must be isostatically contracted (flexed without moving) throughout the motion. Don't be surprised if your glutes are sore the next day.

Another good exercise is one you can do almost anywhere, even when you can't make it to the gym: the basic push-up. The push-up is a good strength-training exercise for the upper body, chest, and abs. The basic push-up will build and keep upper-body strength on point as you get older. Push-ups work the triceps, pectoral muscles, and shoulders; in addition, they can also strengthen the lower back and the core muscles. Push-ups are a fast and effective exercise for building and maintaining strength. I also recommend pull-ups. Maybe you can do one or two pull-ups. It's easy to work your way up into doing more reps. For example, you can get a buddy to hold your legs as you struggle for the extra pull from two reps. Another assist for pull-ups is to use a workout band—put one end on the pull-up bar and the other end over your knee with your knees bent like a sling. It is a great way to assist you in pushing through those extra reps. Good strength- and resistance-training exercises like pull-ups can also improve your overall physical health. Studies have found that regularly performing strength training may help reduce visceral fat and help you manage type 2 diabetes.

In addition, strength training can help improve a man's mental health. In a 2010 review from the NIH, studies found a positive correlation between strength training and the following: reducing anxiety symptoms, improving cognitive function, reducing fatigue, reducing depression, and improving self-esteem (Westcott, 2012).

According to the NIH, inactive adults experience a 3/8-percent loss of muscle mass per decade, accompanied by resting metabolic-rate reduction and fat accumulation. Ten weeks of resistance training may increase lean weight by 1.4 kg, increase resting metabolic rate by 7%, and reduce fat weight by 1.8 kg. Benefits of resistance training include improved physical performance, movement control, walking speed, functional independence, cognitive abilities, and self-esteem. Resistance training may assist prevention and management of type 2 diabetes by decreasing visceral fat, reducing HbA1c, increasing the density of glucose transporter type 4, and improving insulin sensitivity. Resistance training may enhance cardiovascular health by reducing resting blood pressure, decreasing low-density lipoprotein cholesterol and triglycerides, and increasing high-density lipoprotein cholesterol. Resistance training may promote bone development, with studies showing a 1/3-percent increase in bone-mineral density. Resistance training may be effective for reducing lower back pain and easing discomfort associated with arthritis and fibromyalgia and has been shown to reverse specific aging factors in skeletal muscle.

Finally, the squats in this particular exercise can strengthen the leg muscles, core, and back. All these are basic structures that help with mobility and balance. As one grows older, it gets difficult to maintain mobility and balance, which is where strong muscles and doing regular squats should help. Leg-strength exercises are critical for maintaining mobility as we age, says Robert Newton, Ph.D., an exercise researcher at Ball State University. In a 2002 study, Australian researchers saw a correlation between maximal lower-body strength and the length of time it took healthy older men to complete a simple obstacle course. The weakest men took an average of 30% longer to complete the most challenging part of the course, compared to the old-timers who could lift the most. In addition, squats help you stimulate the release of a large growth hormone—testosterone. This hormone is helpful for burning fat, building muscle, and improving strength. The squat is an exercise that loads the bones heavily and thus stimulates the bones to get dense.

You work your calves, quadriceps, hamstrings, glutes, core, and a portion of your back when you perform squat exercises. This provides overall benefits instead of just strengthening one isolated area like leg extensions. Squatting is a fantastic exercise for working multiple muscle groups because of this.

Chapter 5: Testosterone

As we get older, our testosterone levels lessen and may decline gradually 1% per year after age 30 (Healthline, n.d.). What does testosterone do to a man? Testosterone is a sex hormone that plays an important role in the male body. It is expected to regulate sex drive/libido as you get older, handle bone mass, deal with fat distribution, help with muscle mass, and build strength. It also assists in the production of red blood cells and sperm. What happens when a man's testosterone levels are low? According to Medical News Today.com, if a male has a low level of testosterone, the symptoms can include erectile dysfunction, hair loss, and reduced bone mass and sex drive. The hormone has many important functions, especially for younger men going into puberty, including the development of the bones and muscles, the deepening of the voice, hair growth, and other factors related to appearance.

A great way to test your testosterone level is to get an at-home testosterone level test kit by Everlywell. The Everlywell at-home testosterone test kit checks your testosterone level from the convenience of your home, saving you an expensive trip to the doctor's office. The kit is affordable and easy to follow. You can find them at any local drugstore. Everlywell can get your test results back either by mail or email. All it took was six easy steps: writing my information on the saliva tube, then spitting in the tube, tightly closing the tube, and placing the tube in a biohazard bag, then sealing it and mailing it. It was that simple. The instructions were easy to read and to understand.

When your results arrive, they will let you know if your testosterone level is low enough to take additional measures to increase your testosterone levels, such as adding vitamins to your diet, or recommend that you go see your primary-care provider for additional medical examination. I was happy to get my results back; they showed a normal reading range of my testosterone levels for a man my age. It let me know what I was doing with attention to dieting and exercising to maintain good health as I get older.

I choose to monitor my testosterone levels because, as I've gotten older, I have noticed a slight difference in my mood and desire for sex when I am hanging out with my girlfriend. I tend to be grumpy at times, making it difficult for her to be around me. I started a daily routine so I could be healthy and wouldn't be grumpy all the time while I was with her.

At the same time, I was aware of the tendency for men's testosterone levels to decline with age. Therefore, I wanted to confirm for myself that my levels were appropriate for my age group. Additionally, if you have low testosterone levels, it can impact your bodily systems, such as mood, bone density and muscle mass, sex drive, memory loss, and the capacity to achieve and sustain an erection.

Testosterone is important because it is a sex hormone men need that plays important roles in the body. It gives men the ability to control their libido, or desire for sexual activity; bone mass, which influences bone metabolism indirectly through a variety of cytokines and growth; and regulation of body composition, strength, and muscle mass. It also promotes the production of sperm and red blood cells, allowing a small amount of circulating testosterone to be converted to estradiol, which is a form of estrogen.

My daily routine is working. I try to stay conscious of these things. The main focus of my diet is to stay away from fast foods and keep my mind sharp by reading every day for at least 30–45 minutes, either in the morning or at night before bed. Sitting down to read is a good way to create some type of a habit at a certain time of day and to keep your mind sharp. In an article published by Healthline.com, people who read often have reduced stress and enhance sleep to improve memory circuits, while sharpening decision-making skills and, possibly, delay the onslaught of dementia.

Chris Finley

It is genuinely harder for kids from eighteen to twenty. When I was a kid, roughly speaking, the kind of rough patch for my life was probably fourteen to seventeen or something like that. Now, I think it's eighteen to twenty-five, something like that. And I think the reason for that is, all the jobs that the bloody hippies complained about being doomed to in the 1960s have now disappeared. Their problem was, Oh My God! I'm gonna have to go work for a corporation and get a salary for the rest of my life. You know, I'll just end up in it with a pension and that'll be my whole life. It's like, well, it seems like a lot better deal than an endless round of part-time Starbucks jobs. So, you know, some of it is that it's just there's a space now in our culture that's lacking for people to make that transformation from adolescence into adulthood, and so it's just the cost of that is to stall. It's not a good thing, it's not a good thing.

–Jordan Peterson

Chapter 6: Education

For most young men fresh out of high school, college isn't the first thing on your mind. I mean, let's face it: College isn't for everyone. Going to a four-year university can be daunting—the scheduling, the requirement to have certain documents needed to even register—and that is just the beginning of the process. The outrageous cost for a four-year college degree can be limiting. If you want to become a doctor or a lawyer or some type of engineer, you'll need a university degree to get you into those fields—there's no way around it. You're gonna have to go through the process of years of studying; after all, you wouldn't want a doctor who only had one year of anatomy classes and watched YouTube channels about surgeries to operate on you, would you? The opportunities to pursue these high-level career fields are there, but it's gonna take some time.

A few young men will get a boring, dead-end job until they figure out their next move. My recommendation for you younger guys who have been out of high school for a few years or in your mid-to-late 20s is to look into going to a trade school. Some courses are only 12–18 months long, depending on what program you are interested in. It's a great way to get some type of training skills under your belt so you can obtain a better-paying job. Some trade-school graduates earn much higher wages than people might expect. By working in a niche field—depending on what trade you train in— you can make as much money as a four-year degree graduate. On average, a trade-school graduate will make about $42,000 per year. Over the course of 30 years, the difference between that graduate and the 4-year college graduate is only about $90,000. Trade-school graduates also enter the workforce 2 years earlier, thereby getting an extra 2 years' worth of salary. According to an article in the Career Colleges & Schools of Texas website, if you decide to go to trade school, you can spend less than half the cost of a 2–4-year university. And you can work part-time while attending the trade school.

Trade schools are good for the average guy who just wants to get on with his life and grow up a little. Trade schools offer shorter programs by eliminating the extra classes you would take at a two-year community college or a four-year college and letting you focus on the program that interests you the most with hands-on experience and learning. Most students can start working immediately after they finish their program.

If your goal is to get some type of college degree, but you don't want to spend four years in college, there's always your local community college. Most community colleges are very affordable because they are supported by the state, making the cost of tuition very low per class course. Plus, you can take up to four classes at your own pace. Community colleges aren't like most major universities, where you're required to take a full load of four to five classes to be considered or recognized as a full-time student. In addition, community college is a good ideal for older men—anywhere from your 20s to your 40s—who are either looking to change careers or to finally start a career.

If you're an older guy in his prime and you haven't decided on what you want to do, I'm going to guess you have some problems and you need to work through or on some type of drug or alcohol. According to the Center for Behavioral Health Statistics and Quality (CBHSQ), substance abuse remains a behavioral health problem among young adults aged 18–25. In 2022, there were an estimated 35.6 million young adults aged 18–25 in the US. Of these young adults, more than one-third reported binge-drinking alcohol in the past month; about one-fifth of young adults used an illicit drug in the past month (CBHSQ, n.d.).

If you drink or use any type of substance, it may be the reason you haven't made a decision about or haven't done anything with your life. And the reason why you can't think of anything you want to do in your life. That's probably why it's difficult for you to get off your ass and pursue the things you want to do with your life. As a young- or even middle-aged man, you should already be in the beginning stages of your midcareer or further along in some type of career environment. Being on drugs and alcohol on a regular basis can fog your thinking and kill any motivation you might have to want to do something more. Marijuana can cloud your senses and judgment. It can also make it harder to focus, learn, and remember things.

Alcohol at low-to-moderate doses affects decision-making in the social domain and promotes utilitarian decisions over ethical principles (deontological). This is consistent with short-sighted information processing and salient social cues in shaping decisions made under the influence of alcohol. A better understanding of these effects is important to understand altered social functioning during alcohol intoxication. This comes from a study done in Neuropsychopharmacology about the acute effects of alcohol on social and personal decision-making (Karlsson, et al, 2021).

I had a close friend who smoked pot on a regular basis. He always complained that he couldn't seem to get his life together and nothing seemed to go his way. When I suggested to him maybe he should lay off pot smoking so he could clear his head, he got angry and told me that pot wasn't his problem because he could function by going to work every day. He wanted better for himself and didn't know why he couldn't think or take action on his next move for that something better. He didn't realize that he was a functioning pothead who was only doing what was routine—like how you can teach a trained monkey to do the same thing on a daily schedule. In addition, marijuana can also cause changes in mood, amnesia, depersonalization, and disorientation. When smoking pot, you might find it harder to concentrate or remember things. You may find that sleeping is difficult, and you feel depressed.

When he finally took my advice to stop his weed smoking, he started to feel happier about himself within 2–3 weeks. He became more enthused about life and had an idea of what he wanted to do with his life. My friend is currently in his last few months at EMT school training. He was able to juggle his schedule between working as a warehouse stocker and classes. I'm very happy that he has found his path and is more positive about his life.

Chapter 7: The Armed Forces

I know many of you have heard horror stories about joining the military or have family or parents who are against the idea of becoming a soldier. Either you come from a very religious environment, or you have family members that don't want their son or daughter to go through what they went through. The information I'm providing is only an option, so you're aware of other opportunities that are out there for young men as you progress through this world. I am neither suggesting nor recruiting anyone to join the military. I am only providing you with information about what the military has to offer for informational purposes, just to be clear on my agenda. If you would like additional information about the military, please contact your local recruiter or log on to any of the Armed Services' websites.

Joining the military can be a great way to jump-start your on-the-job skills and work history as well as prepare you for the real world. They not only feed you three meals a day, but you are doing the training as your daily work. Contrary to what most people think, being in the military is like having a 9–5 job. The only time you may be working outside those hours is during training. Being in the military, you build lifelong friends and a brotherhood that you will always be a part of. Depending on your job or what branch you join, there's opportunity for travel while receiving an income. Now, you won't make a whole lot of money, but the military does offer highly competitive pay and benefits packages that make up for it, such as the GI Bill, which will pay full tuition at public colleges/trade schools nationwide for veterans and active-duty members. Housing, room, and board, which includes meals, and health and dental-care insurance as well as substantial life insurance are all included. Joining the military would be good for any young man searching for direction in his life and not sure what he wants to do. It's especially attractive for those who live in an area where there is not much opportunity. You can join for as little as two years and gain a good skill, paid for by the government, or/and receive the benefit of the G.I. Bill for college or a trade school. This is a great way for someone fresh out of high school or in their early-to-mid-20s and not sure of what to do with their life.

In addition, when you get out of the military, you are a veteran. There are many businesses that endorse hiring veterans as a good business practice, according to the U.S. Department of Labor (shrm.org, n.d.). They also state that veterans bring several positive attributes and characteristics to the workplace, such as leadership skills, experience working in diverse environments, adaptability, and strong work ethics, to name a few. Another reason most companies prefer to hire a veteran is tax credit. Employers that hire more veterans will see a larger tax credit. The average veteran tax-credit value for companies can be as much as $4,478 for veterans, versus $3,468 for civilians.

According to the Bureau of Labor Statistics, in 2020, 18.5 million men and women were veterans, accounting for about 7% of the civilian, noninstitutionalized population ages 18 and older. ZipRecruiter.com and the Call of Duty Endowment report that veterans are 15.6% less likely than nonveterans job-seekers to be underemployed. In today's competitive market, employers are opening their doors to veterans who bring a wealth of knowledge and skill to the civilian workplace. Organizations gain employees with a wide-ranging experience and competencies when they hire veterans, as shown by the results of a 2017 SHRM

Foundation and National Association of Veteran-Serving Organizations (NAVSO) meeting and studies by the RAND Corporation, Syracuse University's Institute for Veterans and Military Families, and other research institutions.

When I joined the military, it was the best thing for me at the time. I went straight to a four-year college right after high school, where I was not prepared to sit down in a classroom trying to force myself to be disciplined enough to do homework and study for exams. My first year in college I had too much energy, I missed a lot of classes, and hung out with college buddies the majority of the time. Being away from home for the first time was exciting. All this resulted in my getting an academic probation at the beginning of my second year. By the time mid-semester came around, I had already gotten a letter that said I was going to be academically suspended. Realizing I didn't have the patience to continue school at the time and my parents couldn't afford my being suspended and knowing that I didn't want to return home and end up working at McDonalds while waiting to get back into school, I decided to join the military. It was the only way I knew to keep living my life as a free man.

If you don't know what it's like to be free to do what you want to do and live the life you want, you are missing out. Whether you're a single man with no kids or you're a younger man with no responsibility, I advise every man to go out and live your life to the fullest. Explore the world, see what you can accomplish, and become a man on your own merits.

The most successful people share a ferocious obsession with success. They are willing to go wherever necessary to learn new strategies and surround themselves with other successful people.

–Grant Cardone

Chapter 8: Leaving Home

I had a close friend who was in his mid-30s and had never lived away from home. He'd been to the local college near his home, and even had a law degree from a prestigious university, but he always lived near his family. While living in the city he'd known all his life, he was able to obtain a job that offered an average salary for a single man. When it came to dating, his personal life was a roller coaster. None of his relationships ever lasted and rarely resulted in something serious. Even though he enjoyed being close to family, his personal life never managed to pan out. He knew he wanted to get married and have kids but had a hard time meeting women.

One day, when his job decided to let him go, he was forced to move back in with his parents. After applying for several jobs in his city, he realized if he was going to find work he would have to apply out of state. When he got an offer for six figures to move out of state, he was afraid because he had never lived so far away from home. So he decided to take the chance—and the job.

While he lived in another state, he called me almost every weekend for six months. When I spoke to him, he would tell me how depressed he was and that he regretted leaving home. He wished he had stuck it out with his family.

The thing is, my friend had never lived outside of his comfort zone. Once six months went by and he adjusted to his new life, he called and told me he realized the freedom he had in becoming his own man. He felt happier and more confident about living his life away from home and being on his own. It's been almost three years since he moved out of state, and we haven't chatted for eight months besides the occasional texts. The last time I spoke to him on the phone, he had met a woman he liked a lot and whom he had gotten serious about. Being away from home allowed my friend to become the man he was meant to be. He's a reminder to take chances to explore the world and build character.

Character improves certain good or useful traits in a person's character, especially self-reliance, endurance, and courage.

–Collins Dictionary

Sometimes you have to leave home to find the success you're looking for, even if it inconveniences you.

I get it: Some of you can't fathom the idea of leaving home or living in another state away from your family. The truth is, it's your duty as a man to go explore the world. To see what you can accomplish, find what excites you. To see what new lands, people, or environments you can experience. You want to go do your own thing. But you can't seem to get over any doubts that you're doing the right thing. What if you fail or come back too soon and the people who doubted you will say, "I told you so"? That's just it—when things get hard, you keep going. Remember the naysayers and use it as fuel to motivate you to succeed in accomplishing what you're trying to do. Dig in deep, no matter what because it's the only way you are going to be able to prove them wrong.

And believe it or not you will be surprised at how many people close to you will be happy you're trying to do something on your own. And even if you're going through a tough time starting your new life, your friends and family won't see the difficulties. They'll see the success.

Although leaving home was difficult for me at first, after nine months, I came to the realization that I had to do this on my own because I was not going back under any circumstances. And I had to be on my own to do the things I wanted to do. Having the freedom and space to do what I wanted was priceless. Even if I tried, I could not move back home. It would be like letting a wolf run loose in the forest and then putting him back in his cage. And yeah, sometimes certain responsibilities can be scary, but staying right where you are is worse.

Chapter 9: The Point I Want to Make

After being divorced for five years, I found myself in limbo, unsure of what to do with myself or what direction I wanted to go in. I soon realized I didn't have the companionship I used to have, the person I used to base my decisions around. A lot of men in my position run into this roadblock as to what to do with their lives—especially after a divorce and/or when entering their 40s. For most men in the US who end up going through a divorce, they will have nothing to show for all the years spent with their significant other. Nothing but child-support payments, alimony, and extensive bills from their lawyer. They will have wasted the prime of their life with a woman they put first in everything they did, and they lived their life often dictated by their spouses' decisions. And now that the marriage has ended, they will have no idea of who they really are as a man or where they want to be in their life. Most men will have lost themselves within the cycle of marriage and family.

The average age for divorced men in the US, according to Divorce Statistics, which includes divorce rate, race, and marriage length, is 45.5 years of age. Unfortunately, for most men, this comes at a time when they must grow into the next phase of their life—adult manhood. What a man does in his 40s—whether he is married or not—will determine his outcome when he turns 50. I believe if a man is not careful, he will become lost in society and end up drinking and alone the more he comes into this age range. If he's not careful, his life will change for the worse.

When I first encountered this so-called crisis in my 40s, I didn't see it as a crisis; I saw it as just the way it is, as an opportunity. As a man, I was expected to handle my issues diligently. But I realized this was a chance to be a better version of me. A chance to be a better man. While I went through my divorce process, which took several months to complete, I dealt with a lot of emotions that came with it. I couldn't help but think, *what do I do now*? Honestly, after being with my wife for so many years, I had become settled and was mostly basing my life around hers. The fire that I'd had prior to meeting my wife had died. And the desire to meet someone new never crossed my mind.

Unlike women, who seem to start their new lives as quickly as hopping back on a bike after years of not riding, men have a harder time resonating with, and re-entering, society. For most men, this social crisis will make or break them. For me it started to break me; I began drinking often and watched too much television to pass the time. The friends I'd had were mostly her friends. And the friends I'd had prior to meeting my wife had either moved away, moved on, or I let them go over the years while I was living the married life.

Starting over and making new friendships as an older man isn't as easy as when you were in your 20s and in college. Things are different and your only friends now are your coworkers. As I spiraled down this path of nowhere, I realized there is not much information out there to help men maneuver through life both while single and after marriage. But there are a whole spree of articles and books for women on how to be a strong, independent woman with kids.

In my journey to find myself, I hit a lot of emotional roadblocks. It's a wonder I could pick myself up at all. After being accustomed to having one woman in my life, it was hard to transition back into my alter ego, "Mac Daddy" mode (meeting girls again). It's like you have to find your mojo again, and all you need is that one attractive woman to show you just the littlest attention to let you know you may still have it. I toiled away at finding my identity again. At first, the toxic amount of constant alcohol drinking and flirting with women was nothing compared to what I was used to prior to marriage. I began gaining weight, which I contribute to fast food and never being at home enough to listen to my own thoughts.

Even though there is no right or wrong way to pull out of your slump and figure out what to do with your life, the main thing is that you pull out of it. You lick your wound for as long as it takes to get yourself on your feet again and hold your head up high. If you've ever heard the quote that nothing lasts forever and your feelings come and go—well, that's what we have to do as men: give it time. It may not seem like it, but time really does heal all wounds. You will realize you are stronger than you thought as a result of what seemed to be an emotional torment. And looking back at what you went through will seem like nothing in the present.

Although most men are more established in their later years, going through a divorce can disrupt the routine they had created for themselves while married. And bouncing back to create a new life for themself with a partner takes time for most men, depending on the circumstances or what he had to go through when the relationship ended. Even if some guys have to go through a series of one-night-stands, an unending supply of attractive women who are looking for a distinguished man with whom to engage their sexual pleasures, and experienced sexual exploits, the reality for a divorced man is more often filled with him relearning how to live alone or figuring out how to parent as a single father (if he has kids with his ex-spouse) and sitting around wondering what he did wrong in his marriage. The newly single man hopes to learn from the mistakes he made and to work on himself so he can have a better relationship in the future.

In my journey from being married to becoming divorced, I spent the first few years after my divorce wanting to be married again and hoping to find someone new—only to figure out I wasn't ready for another relationship that leads to marriage. The more I thought about it, the more I felt disappointed by the idea of feeling trapped in a situation that made me timid and unsure about what I really wanted for myself.

In this book, I wanted you to understand the different transition men go through. What it takes to grow from a young man into an older man who is trying to find his way through life. I hoped to explain what I went through and what I experienced to help those young men who haven't figured out what they want to do with their lives. To show men how to manage their lives so they don't spiral down into a dead end because they didn't know what they need to know. The price of not knowing makes all the difference in a person's life. I have messed up many opportunities no one told me about until I got older. I hope this book provides you with some good information to assist you, and I hope that you further your research on your own into a career or path that satisfies you.

Conclusion

What motivates young men to leave their homes and venture out? Many boys seem to believe that staying at home and living with their parents is natural. And in some communities, it is. When a young man grows older, he may not leave his parents' home until he is married. If you live with your parents for an extended amount of time, though, this might be disastrous. You won't flourish and mature until you leave your parents' home. You feel self-conscious about being alone when you have responsibilities like paying bills, buying food, and working. You'll be disappointed if you don't.

You need to be confronting the world, confronting challenges, and conquering obstacles. The trouble is, you won't have your mother and father's influence when you strike out on your own. This might lead to resentment from your parents, particularly if you notice them arguing and not getting along. When you don't give your parents room and solitude in your home as an older man, they need to re-establish their bond. They might not say it, or you might not believe them when they claim they don't want you to live on your own. However, this is actually what they want. I say this because I've known people who stayed with their parents for longer than they should have. And then complain about their parents' behavior.

When young men eventually leave home, their attitude toward their parents shifts dramatically. Their animosity toward their parents fades, and they become more grounded and, in their own way, alpha males. However, this transformation can only happen if you live on your own as the man you were born to be. It actually enables us men to confront our anxieties about boredom and loneliness. As a result, you will be able to face your thoughts and gain a better understanding of yourself. If you want to survive, you'll have to confront life on your own. But, eventually, you pick up on things and begin to rely on some of the fundamental principles your parents instilled in you.

Nevertheless, it's all part of growing up, and it gives you the chance to explore your own life and do your own thing without others' opinions of you or feeling like you have to look over your shoulder.

I hope you enjoy reading this book as much as I enjoyed writing it.

About the Author

My name is Chris Finley, and I really love educating people on how to stay motivated about themselves and live the life of their dreams, their passions, and their businesses.

Do Not Go Yet: You Have One Last Thing to Do

If you enjoyed this book or found it useful, I'd be very grateful if you'd post a short review and tell a friend about the book. Your support does make a difference, and I read all the reviews personally to get your feedback and make this book even better.

Thanks again for your support!

References

Cassata, C. (2021, June 8). *10 Areas That Mindfulness & Meditation Make Us Better*. Psych Central. https://psychcentral.com/blog/surprising-health-benefits-of-mindfulness-meditation

CBHSQ. (n.d.). *National Survey on Drug Use and Health* (NSDUH). https://www.samhsa.gov/data/data-we-collect/nsduh-national-survey-drug-use-and-health

DiDonato, T. Ph.D. (2014, January 10). *5 Reasons Why Couples Who Sweat Together, Stay Together*. Psychology Today. https://www.psychologytoday.com/us/blog/meet-catch-and-keep/201401/5-reasons-why-couples-who-sweat-together-stay-together

Employing Military Veterans, *SHRM Business case study*. Shrm.org. https://www.shrm.org/resourcesandtools/tools-and-samples/toolkits/pages/militaryreadyemployer.aspx

Hinchman, W. (2021, March 22). *Deadlifts: 5 Proven Benefits Of Deadlifts That Will Improve Your Performance.* Swolverine.com. https://swolverine.com/blogs/blog/benefits-of-deadlifts

Karlsson, H., Persson, E., Perini, I. Yngve, A. Heilig, M. Tinghög, G. (2021, November 8). Acute effects of alcohol on social and personal decision making. Nature.com. https://www.nature.com/articles/s41386-021-01218-9

Levinson, D. (1978). *The Seasons of a Man's Life.* Ballantine Books.

7 reasons to consider trade school over a 4-year college. ccst.org. https://ccst.org/7-reasons-to-consider-trade-school-over-a-4-year-college/#:~:text=On%20average%2C%20a%20trade%20school,college%20graduate%20is%20only%20%2490%2C000.

Severson, A. (2018, November 7). *Testosterone Levels by Age*. Healthline.com https://www.healthline.com/health/low-testosterone/testosterone-levels-by-age#women

Westcott, W.L. (2012, July–August). *Resistance training is medicine: effects of strength training on health*. National Library of Medicine (NIH) https://pubmed.ncbi.nlm.nih.gov/22777332/

What I Know Now